D0582040

SCOTCH IN MINIATURE

A Collector's Guide
by
Alan Keegan

*New and extensively
revised edition*

Illustrations by Mairi Hedderwick

Northern Books
by Famedram

ISBN 0-905489-60 8
© Copyright 1982, 1984, 1986, 1996 and 2001
Famedram Publishers and Alan Keegan

Contents

8

Introduction to Fourth Edition

In preparing the text for its new format, it has been necessary to make some radical changes to the emphasis of this work. This edition is addressed primarily to the collector of Scotch whisky miniatures.

Most collectors have an interest in the objects of his collection beyond mere possession. One aim of this wee book is to provide background information for the collector of miniatures of Scotch whisky.

Miniature versions of their products were originally issued by liquor companies in order to promote sales of the larger bottles. The practice started in the United States early in the twentieth century and became widespread thereafter the repeal of prohibition. Proprietors of the major blends of Scotch whisky used this method of product promotion from the early thirties.

Promotion of blended Scotch is no longer the only reason for issuing miniatures. They are used to publicise other products and are widely sold as tourist mementoes. They are also produced and sold as collectibles *per se*.

The number of miniatures of Scotch whisky now available is so great that it is no longer practicable to attempt a complete listing. Collectors of Scotch in miniature needing to decide how best to direct their purchasing will find many suggestions for specialising in the following pages.

ALAN KEEGAN
AVIEMORE

Acknowledgements

In writing and revising this book, I have been helped by many friends in the whisky trade. At various times, assistance has been sought from and freely given by David Urquhart of Gordon and MacPhail and Frank Clark of the Cairngorm Whisky Centre.

I have consulted with many collectors, notably Mike Barbakoff, Derek Taylor, Alex Barclay and Gary Dempster. David Hamilton of the Mini Bottle Club has been very helpful and has made his collection of labels available for reproduction. Any errors that may have occurred are my own unaided responsibility.

I am grateful to the late Jack Richmond of Newtonmore, who cheerfully permitted me to plunder his great store of knowledge on all aspects of Scotch whisky.

My wife has suffered long while I struggled with fact and syntax. To her and to the spouses of all committed whisky folk, whether collectors or imbibers, this book is dedicated.

· Laphroaig ·

Some History

The first record of a spirit distilled in Scotland from malted barley was in 1494 but the earlier story of *usquaebaugh* is unknown. It seems likely that knowledge of distilling came to Scotland from Ireland some centuries before that first record. The earliest 'named' whisky was Ferintosh, from the village in Ross-shire where Duncan Forbes of Culloden earned government protection for a distilling operation in the late seventeenth century.

During the eighteenth century, high taxation encouraged illicit distilling, particularly in the more remote districts of the counties of Banff and Inverness. The modern era of the whisky industry dates from 1823 when the Whisky Act made legal distilling more profitable than smuggling. Shortly afterwards a practical continuous still was patented, leading to the growth of the big Lowland grain distilleries. Later in the nineteenth century, the absence from the English market of brandy through decimation of the French vineyards opened the way for the expansion of whisky sales.

In the middle years of the nineteenth century, grain and malt distilleries sold their products independently. The idea of mixing different whiskies was first applied to malts, eg in Usher's 'Old Vatted Glenlivet'; from this it was only a short step to mixing the cheap (but rather bland) grain whiskies with the more expensive flavourful malts. Soon, the great whisky barons, Haig, Buchanan, Dewar and Mackie, who were entrepreneurs of blended whiskies rather than distillers, took over the destinies of the Scotch whisky trade.

Casks, sometimes as small as five gallons in capacity, were the first containers of whisky. Merchants sold to dram shops and inns in large stoneware jars which were often protected by an outer basket of wicker. The dram shops catered for the 'carry out' trade by filling customers' own flagons or jugs. It was only late in the nineteenth century, when the big blending houses developed their own brand names, that the bottling of whisky became common.

Even in the earliest days of the trade it is likely that small bottles were filled as samples. There is a record of the finding of a labelled medicine type bottle of Glen Grant under the floor of the town hall in Rothes, apparently left there by the builders in 1900. The

issuing of miniature bottles as we know them developed in the United States. Triffin *(see page 79)* lists a miniature Bourbon Whiskey named 'Fulton' dating from about 1910.

Collecting Miniature Whiskies

An interest in miniature Scotch whiskies usually comes from a desire to collect and display them rather than from the expectation of enjoying their contents. The new collector, faced with a long list of available miniatures, may be discouraged if his budget is small and space for display is limited. Fortunately, there is scope for specialising, so that a collection of as few as a dozen miniatures may have real significance, if buying has been purposeful.

If the collector decides to concentrate on malt whiskies, his collection may be built up, as quickly as funds and space allow, by following one of a number of possible paths:

1. Concentrate on 'official' bottlings by the proprietors of the distilleries.
2. Collect a miniature from each distillery
3. Expand to collecting each strength and age available.
4. Concentrate on the products of a particular merchant.
5. Buy any miniature containing malt from a particular distillery or group. *(Suggestions for specialisation will be found in the section beginning on page 49)*

Because of the now sometimes bewildering profusion of labels, blended whiskies are not so easily divided into categories. However, some degree of specialisation is possible:

6. Collect 'true' miniatures only *(see page 16)*
7. Confine your interest to miniatures produced by blending companies with their own product label.
8. Specialise in miniatures used for product promotion *(see page 27)*.
9. Seek out commemorative labels *(see page 30)*

The keen collector will graduate from haunting specialist retailers to swapping, to bidding through club auctions *(see page 79)* or to purchasing older collections.

It is a recurrent theme of this book that when a miniature is added to a collection, an interest in the nature of its contents (even though they remain untasted) must add enjoyment to what might otherwise be a sterile process.

Specialisation aids research into the special character of the whisky and the background to its production. The knowledge gleaned will add significance to the acquisition, beyond the appearance of the bottle and its label.

Definitions

MALT WHISKY is produced from malted barley in pot stills. The process is intermittent, one batch being completed before the next is put in the still. Modern distilleries may be highly mechanised but they follow closely on traditional methods, so that each distillery produces a whisky of uniquely distinctive character. When bottled on its own, the product of a distillery is a single malt.

VATTED MALTS blend the products of two or more malt distilleries. Labels usually state 'pure malt' or '100% malt'.

GRAIN WHISKY is produced by a continuous process in patent stills. A fermented 'wash' of grain (usually maize, but with some malted barley) is fed into the still and the alcohol is collected at the end of the process. The patent still operates at a higher temperature than the pot still and is more efficient; much flavour is lost in the process, so that the whiskies from different grain distilleries have little distinctive individuality. The product of both malt and grain distilleries must be matured in oak casks for three years before the spirit may legally be termed whisky.

BLENDED WHISKY contains both malt and grain whiskies. The proportion of each depends on the requirements of the bottler in respect of cost and quality. Standard blends usually contain about 30% malt whiskies.

True Miniatures

A 'true' miniature is one that fairly reproduces on a small scale the appearance of a standard (70cl) bottle. There is a special satisfaction to be had from possessing these replicas, particularly if the shape of the larger bottle or the design of the label is pleasing or unusual.

The production of a bottle of non-standard shape is expensive. In the field of miniatures, such expense is likely to be incurred only if the bottling is to be very large or very prestigious. Fortunately, the bottling of malt whisky is quite frequently considered to fall into the latter category. Recent miniatures of Balvenie, Cardhu, Dalmore, Balblair and Knockando and the older issues of Bowmore, Oban and Aberlour are fine examples of special shapes replicated in miniature. In 1996, the appearance of the miniatures from Macallan was enhanced by giving them the corked stopper used for a number of years on the standard bottle.

Among blended whiskies, the tendency for 'true' miniatures to be withdrawn in favour of the 'airline' format, noted in earlier editions, has been eased, if not reversed. Most blends come in standard bottles but there are some very handsome bottlings of deluxe whiskies. The elaborate Whyte and Mackay 21 year old is no longer on the market but Dimple, Buchanan deluxe, Dunhill and Old Parr survive among older issues. New introductions are Grouse Gold Reserve, J&B Jet and the very handsomely presented Johnnie Walker Blue Label.

Miniature Bottles, Red Lead and Painting on a Small Scale

It is an interesting and surprising fact that, in its original meaning, the word 'miniature' has nothing at all to do with smallness. The present usage is influenced by the similarity in sound to the Latin word for smaller (minor) and smallest (minimus).

The word 'miniature' comes from the Italian miniate, meaning to paint with minium or red lead. This substance was used as a base for the intricate work of illuminating manuscripts. The term 'miniatura' was subsequently applied to intricately painted small portraits and to any painting on a small scale. It was an easy step from this usage to the present dictionary definition of 'miniature' as *a small or reduced copy of anything*.

Oddly enough, when they refer to miniatures in Italy, they speak not of 'miniatura' but of 'mignon' or 'mignonnette', from the French. Mini bottle collectors in the UK may be interested to know that their counterparts in France are *Collectionneurs Buticulamicrophilistes*.

Proof

Whisky contains water as well as alcohol. When we speak of 'proof', we are concerned with the proportion of alcohol to water in a liquid.

When drawn off at the still, the alcoholic strength of new whisky is between 74% and 64% vol. The product is reduced slightly in strength before being put into casks for maturation at about 63% vol. Since alcohol evaporates more quickly than water, the maturing spirit gradually loses strength, but it is normally necessary to add water before bottling at the standard 40% vol.

In an early test of alcoholic strength, alcohol was mixed with gunpowder and a match applied. The alcohol was under proof if the mixture failed to ignite, over proof if it exploded and 'proof' if it burned with a steady blue flame. When strength came to be measured more scientifically with a hydrometer, the amount over or under proof was measured in degrees, proof being 100° in the old British 'Sikes' system.

If you have no gunpowder and do not possess a hydrometer, it may be handy to know another (safe) way to test the strength of a spirit. There used to be a special container called a 'Proof phial', but a miniature may be used for the purpose. The method is to shake the bottle violently and observe the characteristics of the bubbling that follows. The bubbles are larger, greater in number and last longer when the proof is higher.

Since 1980, when Britain subscribed to the International Organisation of Legal Metrology, we have adopted the continental (Gay Lusac) system in which the alcohol content of a spirit is expressed as a percentage of the total volume of the spirit at 20°C. Under the Sikes system, standard bottling of whisky was at 70° proof. The equivalent today is 40 GL or 40% vol.

Before the First World War, the practice had been to bottle at 75° but the lower strength of 70° proof was imposed on the industry to conserve grain stocks and this is still the standard for blends. Most malts are bottled for export at 43% vol and even on the home market an increasing number now appear at that strength.

Malt whisky is sometimes bottled at higher strengths. 57% vol (100° proof) is the strength most frequently found, but it is no longer unusual for malt whisky to be bottled at the strength at which it matured in the cask. Glenfarclas, with its '105' was one of the first distilleries to enter this market and others have followed. Even such conservative firms as Glenmorangie and United Distillers now offer some of their products at cask strength.

An Inverness firm, now a subsidiary of a major brewer, has long offered for sale malts bottled from the cask 'As We Get It'. At one time their Balvenie, bottled 108.6 proof was the highest strength of any whisky available. However, Gordon & MacPhail's cask strength Clynelish exceeds that strength by almost 10°.

Disappearing Miniatures

Nowadays, commercial considerations lead to the introduction of new brands and to the disappearance of others. Many once familiar miniatures, like Crawford's Five Star, grace only the displays of long established collectors. Other blended whiskies which were listed in the first (1982) edition and which are now quite unobtainable, include Benmore, Glayva, Glenfoyle, Jamie Stewart, Macgregor's, Mcleay Duff, Red Hackle, Something Special and Usher's Old Vatted.

Occasionally there are surprise re-appearances. Haig Dimple, for example, had been off the domestic market for a number of years when it was reintroduced to promote the launch of the 12 year old bottling.

Because of the modern fashion for periodic changes of image to please consumer demand, some labels now stay on the market for a relatively short time. A few malts, for example Macallan, Knockando and, for a time, Auchroisk, have been labelled with the year of distillation rather than age. Earlier bottlings of these can be hard to find, though the general appearance of the labels have remained the same.

Some miniatures have been produced in fairly small numbers for specific markets The true miniature of the eight year old Dalwhinnie was sold only locally. Other miniatures, being introduced for promotional or for non-commercial purposes, may not be available to retailers.

Label Language and the Quality of Blends

The description on the label of a miniature whisky may not be a reliable guide to the contents. Before labelling regulations were tightened, details of strength and capacity often went unrecorded. There may be a better known parent company behind the name of the bottler.

Some whisky companies show a remarkable want of modesty when describing their product. The most ordinary blend is 'special', 'choice' or 'the finest'. A product declared on the label to be 'old', 'rare' or even 'old and rare', may be quite young for a whisky. We come to accept these terms as embroidery.

The description 'deluxe' is more reliable, this being applied by whisky companies to their premium (as distinct from standard) blends.

Some blends carry an indication of age on the label. When this occurs, every constituent whisky in the blend must by law have attained that age at the time of bottling. The absence of a stated age does not necessarily mean that the whisky is inferior. The proportion of malt whisky to grain and the quality of the constituent malts are relevant factors; the products of some distilleries are specially prized by blenders and the use of such 'crack' malts as Cragganmore, Glenlivet and Macallan affects the cost – and the quality – of the blend they are used in.

Variants

Many collectors will be content to have just one miniature of each label. Others will want to acquire major variants while the fanatical few will consider even the smallest change in label or bottle format a good reason for adding another miniature to their collections.

BOTTLE SHAPES: Proprietary blends may be issued with the same label in a variety of formats, according to their intended use. Sometimes a standard shaped bottle has been used when a fancy shape has been temporarily unavailable. Examples are: Aberlour, Cardhu, Tormore and, more recently, Old Pulteney

DIFFERENT CAPS: Some miniatures may appear with or without the name printed on the cap. Variations in colour are usually fortuitous

LABEL VARIATIONS: Apart from obvious major design changes, minor label variations can be detected only if direct comparisons are made. There were many instances of variations following the introduction of metric measurements. Some collectors find significance in even small differences in the position of these details on the label.

EXPORT VERSIONS: Local regulations lead to much variety in detail on the labels of exported miniatures: For example, at one count, Dewar's had 63 differently worded labels for their 'White Label' miniatures.

Shapely Bottles, Pretty Labels

That a miniature is pleasing to look at is a good reason for choosing to buy it. A shapely bottle (eg: the Oban 'perfume bottle') or a colourful, well designed label (the Tamdhu burn, the bold stags on Glengarioch and Scottish Leader) may influence the purchase of a miniature as much as the name of the whisky.

For a while in the early nineties, there was a trend towards pictorial labels and colourful views of distilleries abounded. The very pretty 'fauna' series of labels issued by United Distillers for many of their standard malts, have appeared on miniatures for Clynelish, Blair Athol and Aberfeldy only and these have had limited distribution.

One of the prettiest labels is on Cadenhead's Putachieside. Sadly, the original printing plates have been lost and the reissued label does not have the crisp quality of the older one. Another fine illustrated label was that depicting a sailing boat on Sherriff's bottling of Bowmore. The use of semi-transparent labels works well on the true miniature of Old Pulteney with its picture of a fishing boat but is insipid against the pale whisky in the miniature of Isle of Jura.

Perhaps the most startling decorative label is that designed by Ralph Steadman for the 35th anniversary of *Private Eye* and applied to both 70cl and miniature Macallan bottles There could hardly be a greater contrast to the familiar label on the standard Macallan.

Miniatures and Literature

Scottish literature abounds in references to whisky but it would seem that our writers have not been interested in their national drink in small containers, so that we have to turn to an English author for a literary reference to whisky miniatures. Readers of Graham Green's *Our Man in Havana* will recall Wormold's memorable game of draughts with the captain of police. Miniatures were used for counters and the winner of each game drank the contents. It was Scotch vs. Bourbon and it was Scotch that, by losing the game, won the tactical battle.

The book was written in the late fifties and collectors may be interested in the whisky miniatures named: Cairngorm (*an unfamiliar whisky… it found a raw spot on Wormold's tongue*), Dimple, Red Label, Dunosdale Cream, George IV and Old Argyle. The actual miniatures from Graham Green's collection were auctioned in Glasgow in the early nineties; they were mostly flask shaped and some lacked contents.

'Own Label' Miniature Whiskies

The practice by which merchants and others have their own label placed on somebody else's product has become widespread in the field of miniature whiskies. From their nature, these bottlings should be obtainable only from the proprietors of the label. Some of the miniatures that fall into this category contain 'own brand' whiskies, specially blended and bottled for the proprietors. At the other end of the scale there are instances where enterprising collectors have re-labelled a few standard miniatures to create a reserve of exclusive 'swaps'. Between the two extremes, it is not always easy to judge the legitimacy of the labelling. Some of the 'own label' miniatures most likely to be found and most worthy of the attention of collectors, are mentioned below.

STORES: Harrod's have their own bottlings of both blended and malt whiskies and they have miniatures on sale exclusively at their Knightsbridge store. The Scotch House has its own miniature, while Marks and Spencer periodically issue 5cl bottles in presentation packs.

In the early eighties, Lambert Brothers bottled miniatures for a number of stores in the USA. The labels were uniformly dull.

A considerable number of small shops in the north and west of Scotland have their own labels, many placed on the miniatures at a single source.

25

HOTELS: Craw's Nest, Turnberry and Dunkeld House are three hotels with distinctive labels. Inverlochy Castle Hotel* had an interesting miniature, now a collector's piece, of its 'Grand Reserve' whisky. Less distinguished are the many labels, printed uniformly white on green bottles, for smaller hotels and restaurants throughout Scotland by a Kilmarnock firm.

STATELY HOMES: that open their doors to the public: Glamis Castle* and Hopetoun House have had their own miniatures. Cawdor has a blend ('Thane of Cawdor') and a Speyside malt. Visitors to Balmoral may purchase a 15 year old malt miniature with an undistinguished label.

Ballindalloch Castle has bottled several 'vintages' of the malt from a neighbouring distillery for use of guests; miniatures are sold to the public.

The Dalchully* estate in upper Speyside had its own label for a 15 year old Speyside malt. Duff House has a special bottling of MacDuff malt.

The House of Commons blend, bottled by Buchanan's, is one of the most handsome 'own label' miniatures; it is available only at the Palace of Westminster.

CHARITIES: As a contribution to local charities, United Distillers have issued special labels for Dufftown (Cancer Research), Coleburn (Moray scanner appeal) and Clynelish.

These labels are illustrated on page 63

Miniatures Used for Product Promotion

Miniatures used for product promotion are not likely to be found in retail shops. In some cases, they may be sold at the proprietor's premises but, in general, they will be given away at exhibitions or trade fairs and the collector will need some luck to come across them. However, possession of such exclusive miniatures will help lend interest to a collection.

Whisky Companies: Promotion of their product was the prime reason for whisky companies to issue miniature bottles. Some examples of less widely distributed items are given in the Rare Malts section (*see pages 64-67*). Signatory Vintage has distributed some interesting special miniatures at trade fairs

Cashmere Blend: Originally issued to promote a new knitwear venture, this miniature is sold at the company's Elgin visitor centre. The same firm marked its bicentenary with a specially labelled Glenfarclas miniature.

Books: A miniature called 'Love of Scotland' was used at a trade fair to help sell a new book and was later on general sale in tourist shops.

Financial Services: One of the most attractive special labellings was issued on a Macallan miniature, to publicise the services offered by a finance company, ICFC.

British Rail: Several miniatures were used to promote different aspects of British Rail's service, including

'Highspeed Dram', 'Sweet Dreams' and 'Speedlink Dram'.

Most unusual was the miniature planned to promote the Advanced Passenger Train. The label was in the shape of the proposed engine and, being designed to fit a triangular Grant's bottle, was intended to be displayed on its side.

Scotland's For Me: for a season or two, Scotland promoted itself, using its own most famous product. The original flat bottling by Whyte & Mackay was never available for purchase but a later version, using Highland Queen miniatures, was sold through specialist shops.

Miniature Whiskies as Souvenirs

Any Scotch whisky miniature is a fitting 'minding' of a visit to Scotland and many thousands of standard blends and malts are purchased for this purpose each year. Until the mid '80s surprisingly little attempt was made to exploit Scotland's national drink as a souvenir. However, there has now been a proliferation of special labels for particular places and attractions. Not all of these have been well designed and for most of them, the whisky content is incidental.

Gordon & MacPhail pioneered the packaging of malt whisky miniatures with their 'Tartanpaks'. Many others are now marketed in presentation boxes or tubes and make excellent gifts. Some standard blended miniatures have names or labels that are appropriate as souvenirs: Grouse, Isle of Skye, Spey Cast, Hielanman, Thistle and White Heather come to mind.

There is a series of Clan miniatures sold mostly in specialist tartan shops and a few other labels incorporate some tartan in their design. There are kilted figures on Glen Grant and Glen Scotia labels but otherwise Scotch malt whisky labels are free of overt Scottish symbols.

There are few instances of the use of Gaelic on miniature labels. *Té Bheag* is 'The Little Woman' and *Poit Dhubh* is 'Black Pot', the Highlander's name for, respectively, his dram and an illicit still.

Whisky Miniatures for Special Occasions

Royal events had been commemorated on flagons, but the wedding of the Prince of Wales seems to have been the first to be marked by special miniature bottlings. The most popular was in flat 'airline' format with a portrait label. The three malts issued for the same occasion by Gordon & MacPhail were vattings of whiskies distilled in 1948 and 1961, the respective birth years of Charles and Diana. Subsequent royal occasions have been marked by the issue of miniature bottles or flagons.

Anniversaries of firms, clubs, historical events and birth dates have all had their special miniatures: Berlin's 750 years was celebrated on Glenfarclas. *'Siemens in the United Kingdom, 1843-1993'* appeared on a Glenmorangie label. The centenary of the West Highland Railway was commemorated on both a Glengarioch malt and a Dew of Ben Nevis blend. Anniversaries of battles have been commemorated: Inverlochy's 350, Battle of Britain's 50. Births have been remembered, especially the bicentenary of that of Robert Burns. The putative fifth centenary of the whisky industry in Scotland was well marked by miniature labels.

Miniatures from the Morrison Bowmore group and from Springbank have been much used, officially, to mark special occasions. Bowmore 10 year old was specially labelled to mark the Forth Bridge Centennial in 1990. To help celebrate receiving the Queen's Award to Industry in 1994, John Brown Engineering arranged a special bottling of Auchentoshan. In the same year there

was a miniature labelling of Springbank for the
Edinburgh Festival. The previous year, Springbank had
been the appropriate choice for a miniature when the
Ayrshire Cattle Society held a conference in
Campbeltown

Miniatures have been
presented to delegates at some
licensed trade events. Whyte &
Mackay marked the 1981
conference of the Scottish Licensed
Trade Association – and the royal
wedding of that year – with a special
label. In the two following years
delegates received similar souvenirs.

The SLTA conference of 1986 was chaired by
Bell's and those attending were presented with small
white bells bearing an appropriate message.

Clynelish helped mark Embo's 'day of Freedom' in
the summer of 1989 with a special labelling of their malt.
The use of Glengoyne to help celebrate a wedding in
1983 was, like many other limited issues, a re-labelling
exercise.

Label Printing

A stamp collector who takes his hobby seriously will be quick to recognise a stamp that has been issued just for the collector. Having recognised its purpose, he will probably reject it, preferring to collect only those stamps that are issued for postal purposes. Collectors of miniature whiskies are often faced with a similar situation, with new labels being issued only because there are collectors who will buy them.

Sometimes, those that issue such labels find it economic to have a series with a connecting theme. Mr Lambert's 'Munros' and a series of 'mist' miniatures, bearing a reproduction of a painting of the location concerned, had considerable potential for additions.

Another class of label that has appeared on whisky miniatures involves concocted 'brand' names. Many of these incorporate Scots idioms and tourist themes; a good number of them are designed to amuse.

A collector whose hobby is based on a genuine interest in whisky will be selective in his purchasing, knowing that there are sufficient 'legitimate' miniatures on the market to satisfy the collecting urge of most of us.

If a collector finds that he has acquired a suspect label and does not wish to display it, there is a remedy open to him: He can realise the value of his purchase by drinking the whisky. There is no such consolation for the philatelist who acquires a dud stamp!

Jugs, Jars, Flagons and Flasks

In the thirties and early post-war years, a popular souvenir of a visit to Scotland was a miniature stoneware flagon, often filled with an unnamed Scotch whisky and bearing an appropriate message. 'Cheers from Tomintoul' and 'A Wee Deoch an Doras from Braemar' are examples of the genre.

Miniature flagons are still produced and though often bought primarily as novelties, they have historic relevance, being replicas of the kind of domestic vessel used before bottled whisky became the norm.

The Usquaebach miniature is unusual, being a copy of an old two or three gallon storage jar rather than the usual pint flagon.

A miniature of the stylish Glenfiddich 'crock' which was sold without contents, can no longer be bought but the visitor to this most visited of distilleries can buy a distinctive 50ml Wedgwood decanter or, if he can afford it, a tastefully decorated miniature containing 50 year old Glenfiddich, lavishly boxed

Two firms, Rutherford's and Lindisfarne, specialise in the production of miniature flagons for the Scottish souvenir market. They are decorated with transfers depicting a variety of personalities, scenes and themes associated with Scotland.

Novelties and Curiosities

Visitors to Scotland will be aware of the many novelty containers of whisky that are offered for sale in tourist shops. These novelties vary greatly in quality but nearly all have in common the fact that the whisky content is largely irrelevant. Among the best of the figures are the wildlife models originally produced by Wade for Peter Thomson Ltd of Perth and latterly marketed by Whyte & Mackay. Peter Thomson issued 'The Thistle and the Rose' chess set, based on personalities from Scottish and English history.

Bell's decanter in the shape of a hand bell is found in various capacities, including 5cl. A miniature bell was given to their employees to commemorate the wedding of the Prince of Wales has commanded a high price from collectors.

Ceramic novelties have come in a variety of shapes, from footballs to curling stones and from bulls to books. Golfers are a particular target. Replicas of Golf balls, club-heads and bags, tartan or plain, may be purchased;

Another curiosity is the micro-mini or piccolo. One firm in Scotland markets these with various proprietary labels and there is an entry in the *Guinness Book of Records* to substantiate the claim that these are the smallest bottles of whisky in the world.

Displaying Miniatures

Whatever its size, a collection of miniatures can provide a fine feature display. A small collection is easy enough to accommodate but, as more bottles are accumulated, dusting becomes a problem and some sort of enclosed cabinet is desirable. Any glass fronted display shelving may be adapted but a larger collection will justify having cabinets specially made by a local joiner.

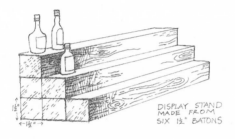

DISPLAY STAND
MADE FROM
SIX 1½" BATONS

Lengths of 40mm x 40mm timber can be used to economise space in shelving. Six cut to the required length will give four tiers on a 150mm wide shelf. With a gap of 300mm between shelves, this arrangement will permit the display of 100 miniatures per metre of shelving. A more sophisticated system may be devised, using 50mm wide plate glass instead of the timber.

Vatted Malt Whiskies

George Sainsbury, whose *Notes on a Cellar Book* is a connoisseurs' classic, would blend different malts in various ways, the better to enjoy the flavours; a mixture of Clynelish and Glenlivet is one he approved. Such do-it-yourself blending is little practised nowadays, but it illustrates the philosophy behind the technique of vatting malt whiskies. In the middle of the nineteenth century the technique began to be used by the 'legitimate' market as a device for 'ironing out' variations between different distillations from the same distillery.

The Edinburgh merchant Andrew Usher who was agent for The Glenlivet, produced the first 'branded' vatted malt. His 'Old Vatted Glenlivet' contained other Speyside whiskies as well as The Glenlivet.

More recent proprietary brands of vatted malts were marketed as part of a balanced portfolio, by companies that either did not have access to or did not wish to promote their own single malt. The four 'Prides' issued by Gordon & MacPhail give an interesting opportunity to taste vatted malts on a regional basis.

The use of terms like 'pure malt' can be ambiguous. It is sometimes impossible to distinguish a vatted malt from a single that has been put out under the bottler's own label.

Single Grain Whisky Miniatures

The output of the large grain distilleries has usually been reserved only for the production of blended whiskies. The sole exception for many years was Haig's 'Choice Old Cameron Brig' which is marketed mainly in Fife. A few 'true' miniatures of this whisky have been available to visitors to the Cameronbridge Distillery and are much prized by collectors. 'Official' miniatures of Port Dundas and Caledonian Grains have been issued for special occasions in small numbers and are difficult to come by. William Grant & Sons have bottled their Girvan grain whisky under the brand name 'Black Barrel'. This can be purchased in miniature form at Glenfiddich Distillery as part of a boxed set of five entitled 'The Spirit of Independence'. In contrast, miniatures of Invergordon Grain have been widely sold since the 70cl bottle was launched in the late 80s.

Strathmore Grain (North of Scotland Distillery) was bottled in miniature by Strachan's of Aboyne, and was fairly widely sold in Scotland for a number of years. Other grain whiskies have been marketed in merchants' bottlings; details appear in the distilleries index.

Scottish Spirit

As part of a promotional exercise, the product of the recently established Isle of Arran Distillery has been marketed and sold in miniature as 'First Production 1995', '1 Year Old Spirit 1996' and '2 Year Old Spirit 1997' Like the product of every other Scottish distillery, this spirit will have to be matured in oak casks for at least three years before it can be sold as Scotch whisky. Springbank included a miniature of 'Plain British Spirit' in a limited set of different ages of their product. Their associated company, Cadenhead's, have issued two versions of 'Triple S' (Single Scottish Spirit), one peated, the other not – presumably representing Longrow and Springbank distillations.

Whisky Liqueurs

During the eighteenth and early nineteenth centuries, local whisky was found in few genteel Scottish homes; ale, wine and brandy were more likely to be used. The practice of maturing whisky in wood to remove the harsher elements was not widespread and the raw product of the Highland stills was largely left to ordinary folk. However, it was found that the rough edge of immature whisky could be disguised by adding fruits, herbs and other flavourings. The toddies and punches that resulted from this discovery are the forerunners of whisky liqueurs.

The first whisky based liqueur to be marketed, and still the most familiar, is Drambuie. The romantic tale of its association with the wanderings of Prince Charles Edward is told on the label. In common with liqueurs the world over, the formulation of Drambuie is a closely guarded secret. Glayva is also widely available and rather similar liqueurs have been marketed under Johnnie Walker, Buchanan's and Glenturret labels.

Wallace liqueur claims no direct association with Scotland's earlier hero; the package lists among the ingredients Deanston malt, Scottish berries and French herbs. Stag's Breath, taking its name from a brand mentioned in Compton Mackenzie's *Whisky Galore*, contains 'fermented comb honey'. 'Cock O'The North' was the by-name of the last Duke of Gordon and is applied to a liqueur marketed by the Gordon family

The origins of Atholl Brose are lost in early Highland history. Brose is prepared by pouring boiling water or milk onto oatmeal: whisky would be a natural additive. The liqueur marketed by Gordon & MacPhail is 'Meg Dodd's Dunkeld Atholl Brose' and contains no oatmeal.

Inspired, perhaps, by the success of Bailey's Irish Cream, a number of rather similar concoctions have been marketed in Scotland – Heather Cream and Columba Cream are the most widely found.

Rather different was Mrs McGillivray's Apple liqueur, a spicy confection, promoted for a while by the owners of Drambuie.

All the liqueurs mentioned have been available in miniature form.

Single Malt Whiskies

The making of malt whisky has been described succinctly by Birnie (1939) as follows:

Clean barley is turned into Malt by Steeping, Germination and Drying. It is then Mashed with hot water, to produce a sweet solution of Malt Extract. Fermentation with Yeast turns the sugar into Alcohol. Distillation is then carried out twice in Pot Stills. The resulting raw Malt Whisky is put into wooden casks to mature.'

Each stage in the production of a particular malt whisky helps the formation of its unique character. The barley chosen, the extent to which peat is used in malting, the source of the process water, the shape of the stills and the selection of the middle cut of each distillation will all have bearing on the taste of the malt whisky when finally it is committed to the bottle. Relevant also will be the type of cask into which the new spirit is filled, the conditions under which the cask is stored and the duration of the maturation period. When finally bottled, without the addition of any grain whisky (which would make a blend) or of a whisky from another malt distillery, it is termed a single malt or, in older parlance, a self whisky.

Since 1945, 119 distilleries have produced malt whisky in Scotland. At least 19 of these have been dismantled and a number of others have been 'mothballed'. The product of most of the distilleries has been bottled in one form or another. Many of the individual bottlings have been done by merchants but in terms of volume, most of the malt whisky sold in bottle is now officially produced and marketed by the owners of the distilleries.

In spite of the increased bottle sales, the market for malt whiskies is relatively small and most of the output of the malt distilleries is still sold in bulk for blending. The best selling blend, Johnnie Walker Red Label, has worldwide sales eight times higher than Glenfiddich, the best selling single malt.

The Age of Malt Whisky

The age of most bottled malt whiskies is stated on the label. As whisky matures only in the wood, the age is that at the date of bottling. Whisky distillers consider that there is a certain age when each malt reaches a peak of maturity, after which that malt will not improve. The age may vary greatly but there seems to be general agreement that Speyside malts reach their optimum maturity at about 15 years but others, especially the lighter malts, will peak at a much younger age. There is a danger that, after a certain time, the influence of the cask will impart a woodiness that may be unpleasant.

Details of age are not always given on the label but the absence of this information does not necessarily indicate extreme youth. Some companies are more concerned with consistency of taste, and will achieve this by mixing different ages of their malt. Glenfiddich is a notable example; even their '1887 Classic' had no age statement on the label but clearly contains well matured Glenfiddich.

The oldest malt whisky made available in bottle is a 1919 Springbank. A limited edition of fewer than two dozen individually numbered miniatures was released in 1985. Gordon & MacPhail have issued a number of 50 year old miniatures, including Glen Grant, Glenlivet and Mortlach, while Glenfiddich has put some of its 50 year old into 5cl ceramic jars. A miniature of the 1947 Macallan was issued in limited numbers by the proprietors in early 2000.

Glenlivet and the Definite Article

When such things mattered more than they do today, the chief of one Highland clan declared that only three people were entitled to place 'The' before their name: The King, The Pope and The Chisholm.

Prefixing the definite article to suggest primacy is a device used to promote several malt whiskies. In recent advertising, Macallan has gone further and styled itself 'The Malt'.

One distillery has gained recognition in law for 'The' before its name. George Smith's Glenlivet Distillery had the distinction of being the first to take out a licence under the Whisky Act of 1823. His whisky gained a great reputation in Victorian times and other distillers sought to share its fame by adding 'Glenlivet' to the name of their own distillery. A lawsuit in 1880 failed to stop this but did win the proprietors the right to the title 'The Glenlivet'. The continued use of the name by others led to advertisements like:

George and John Gordon Smith… beg to intimate that Glenlivet is a district which belongs to his Grace the Duke of Richmond and Gordon, and that their distillery was the first and is now the only licensed distillery in Glenlivet and that they are the sole manufacturers of Glenlivet Whisky

There are now two other distilleries in the glen: Tamnavulin and Braeval, which was originally known as 'Braes of Glenlivet'.

Who Owns What?
Malt Distilleries and Associated Blends

Since Macallan fell to Highland Distillers, Glenfarclas is the only independent distillery whose product cannot be linked directly to a particular blend. Most other distilleries are owned by or closely connected with firms whose principal activity is the production and marketing of one or more brands of blended whisky. In the following lists, distilleries still within each group are shown bold. Some of these may be temporarily or permanently silent (mothballed)

Diageo (United Distillers/IDV/Bell's)

The Scotch whisky industry has been dominated for most of this century by the Distillers Company Limited and its successor United Distillers. The latter was a subsidiary of Guinness Plc who, having absorbed Arthur Bell & Sons in 1986, took control of DCL. Diageo was formed in 1997 by an amalgamation with Grand Metropolitan.

The following distilleries are now within the group: **Benrinnes, Blair Athol, Caol Ila, Cardhu,** **Clynelish, Cragganmore, Daluaine, Dalwhinnie,** **Dufftown, Craigellachie, Glendullan, Glen Elgin, Glen** **Kinchie, Glen Lossie, Glen Ord, Inchgower, Lagavulin,** **Linkwood, Lochnagar, Manochmore, Mortlach, Oban,** **Pittyvaich, Talisker,** and **Teaninich.** Four distilleries joined the group from IDV: **Auchroisk, Glen Spey,** **Knockando,** and **Strathmill.** Dallas Dhu was sold to

Historic Scotland and is now a museum. After the formation of Diageo, the group was obliged to dispose of the Dewar's brand along with Aberfeldy, Aultmore, Craigellachie and Brackla. These now belong to Bacardi. Some distilleries – Balmenach, Knockdhu, Speyburn, Imperial, Glentauchers, and Benromach – have been sold to other whisky companies. Bladnoch is leased out. Other distilleries have been closed: Banff, Brora, Coleburn, Convalmore, Glen Albyn, Glenlochy, Glen Esk, Glenury Royal, Glen Mhor, Millburn, North Port, Port Ellen, Rosebank and St Magdalene. Caledonian, Cambus and Carsebridge, former SGD grain distilleries, are closed but **Cameronbridge, Strathmore** and **Port Dundas** remain within the group

Among the older DCL brands that remain with the new company are: *Abbott's Choice, Ainslie's Royal Edinburgh, Benmore, Bisset's, Black and White, Buchanan's, Chequer's, Crabbie's, Dimple, Haig's, House of Commons, Jamie Stuart, John Begg, Johnnie Walker, King George IV, King of Kings, King William IV, Lord Douglas, Logan's, McCallum's Perfection, Macleay Duff, Old Angus, Old Parr, Old Rarity, Peter Dawson, President, Robbie Burns, Thistle, Usher's, VAT 69, White Horse* and *Ye Monks*

Bell's and Islander came to the group after the take over by Guinness while IDV contributed *Dunhill's, J&B Rare, Royal Ages* and *Spey Royal* to the portfolio of brands.

Allied Distillers

Owners of the second largest group of malt distilleries and incorporating Hiram Walker and Long John Distillers. They purchased **Imperial** and **Glentauchers** from United Distillers but have sold Balblair and Pulteney to Inver House and Ardbeg to Glenmorangie. Kinclaith, which produced malt whisky within the **Strathclyde** grain distillery, was dismantled in the seventies. Other distilleries in the group are: **Ardmore, Glenburgie, Glencadam, Glendronach, Glenugie, Inverleven, Laphroaig, Miltonduff, Scapa** and **Tormore.** The company also owns **Dumbarton** grain distillery and its blends include: *Ballantine's, Old Smuggler, Teacher's, Stewart's Cream of the Barley, Long John* and *Black Bottle.*

Seagram Distillers

The largest producer of alcoholic drinks in the world, they established themselves in the UK market by buying Chivas Brothers in 1949. The take over of Glenlivet Distillers in 1978 brought the total of malt distilleries under Seagram's ownership to nine: **Allt A'Bhainne, Benriach, Braeval (Braes of Glenlivet), Caperdonich, Glen Grant, Glen Keith, Glenlivet, Longmorn** and **Strathisla.** Their best known blends are: *Passport, 100 Pipers, Chivas Regal, Royal Salute, Queen Anne, St Leger* and *Something Special*

Glenlivet.

American Brands

Through their take over of Whyte & Mackay and Invergordon, this firm acquired nine malt distilleries (Ben Wyvis was already dismantled). Of the nine Deanston and Speyburn have been sold, leaving **Bruichladdich, Dalmore, Fettercairn, Isle of Jura, Tamnavulin, Tomintoul** and **Tullibardine**. *Scots Grey, Whyte & Mackay, Mackinlay's, Cluny* and *Findlater's* are blends marketed by the enlarged company.

Highland Distillers

They now control **Bunnahabhain, Glenglassaugh** (mothballed), **Glenrothes, Glenturret, Highland Park, Macallan** and **Tamdhu,** distilleries. *Famous Grouse* and *Cutty Sark* are among Highland Distillers blends. **Glengoyne** owned by Robertson & Baxter is associated with Highland Distillers. They sell *Lang's* blends.

Pernod Ricard own **Aberlour, Edradour** and **Glenallachie.** They bottle *White Heather, Clan Campbell, King's Ransom* and *House of Lords* blends.

William Grant & Sons own *Grant's Standfast* and *Robbie Dhu* blends. They have a grain distillery at **Girvan** within which Ladyburn malt distillery (closed in 1975) was housed. Their flagship distillery is **Glenfiddich** and they also own **Balvenie** and **Kininvie**.

Morrison Bowmore

This firm, now a subsidiary of the Japanese whisky giant, Suntory, owns **Bowmore, Auchentoshan** and **Glengarioch** distilleries. *Rob Roy* is one of their blends.

Glenmorangie (formerly Macdonald & Muir) operates **Glenmorangie, Glen Moray** and **Ardbeg** distilleries. They market *Highland Queen, Muirhead's, John Martin* and *Bailie Nicol Jarvie* blends

Inver House, who once operated a grain distillery at Moffat, where Glen Flagler malt was also made, have in recent years acquired six distilleries discarded by larger companies: Knockdhu (renamed **An Cnoc**), **Speyburn** and **Balmenach** from United Distillers; **Balblair** and **Pulteney** from Allied. The *Hankey Bannister* and *Catto's* brands have been purchased from IDV.

Other multiple owners are:

<u>Bacardi</u>, as already mentioned, acquired **Aberfeldy, Aultmore, Craigellachie** and **Royal Brackla** from Diageo, along with the *Dewar's* brand name.

Burns Stewart own **Deanston** and **Ledaig** (Tobermory). They market *Scottish Leader* and *Burberry* blends.

Loch Lomond Distillers own **Glen Scotia, Littlemill** and **Loch Lomond** distilleries.

Two distilleries belong to Japanese groups: **Tomatin** (Takara & Ikura) and **Ben Nevis** (Nikka). **Macduff** belongs to Martini Rossi while the now closed Lochside Distillery belonged to a Spanish firm. Ben Nevis and Lochside also produced grain whisky.

Five distilleries may be described as independent: **Drumguish** (Speyside Distillery Co), **Glenfarclas** (J & G Grant), **Isle of Arran**, **Springbank** and **Benromach** (Gordon & MacPhail).

Collecting Malt Miniatures

Only another 112 to go.............

In previous editions of this book, an attempt was made to list all the malt whiskies that have been issued as miniatures, with all variations of bottle shape and label design. This is no longer practicable. In the index of distilleries, given at the end of the book, there is an indication of the scale of bottlings in miniature both by the owners of the distilleries and by independent merchants.

Proprietary Malt Miniatures

Single malts, bottled by the owners of the distillery, are the most attractive field within which a collector might specialise. After acquiring a specimen from all available distilleries, the collector may then wish to concentrate his collecting zeal on a particular distillery or group. Details of labels issued and some suggestions for specialising are contained in the following pages.

49

Aberlour The scroll label (a) appeared on a square bottle

at 8 (in Italy where the label also appeared on a tall round miniature), 9 and 12 year old. The latter also had a modified version.

a   b

A 'VOHM' issue was in the style of a brandy bottle. Later standard round miniatures have had variations of label (b), with a tower motif.

Ardbeg: The miniature of the 10 year old has not been available for some time but the same style of label has been retained on the 17 year old issued after the distillery was acquired by Glenmorangie

Auchentoshan. Two versions of a black label with gold 'still' (a, b) were followed for a while by a cream one (c) which was abandoned in favour a lozenge shape (d), colour coded for different ages of the contents:

a   b   c   d

Auchroisk: Just one label has been used with variations only to show the year of distillation: 1975, '76, '78, '81, '83 and '85. A 10 year old was introduced later.

Balvenie: After the original matt black label found on the flat 8 year old, there were a number of miniature in brandy bottle shapes (a) below followed by 'true' miniatures of 10, 12 and 15 year old malts with plain labels.

a b c

Bladnoch: Before Bell's introduced label (b) above, there was a plainer one (c) also depicting the distillery.

Blair Athol and **Dufftown** had similar labels under Bell's proprietorship. The sombre label with a drawing of the distillery in a vignette (a, b) was followed in·the eighties by a *cartouche* design (c) and finally by bright colourful pictorial labels (d). United Distillers 'fauna' label has appeared on a Blair Athol miniature.

a b c d

Bowmore: Under Sherriff's ownership, there were two 'true' miniatures; a 7 year old with a view of the distillery and the handsome 'sailboat' label. Morrisons introduced the brown 'still' shaped bottle with label (a). During the nineties, several labels have been issued with 'seagull' motif (b, c, d) with colour bands indicating different ages.

a b c d

Bruichladdich: The early design (a) received a heavy gold border in the early nineties and was replaced successively by a cleaner label (b) and by a partially transparent one incorporating a seascape and showing the longitude of the most westerly of the Scottish distilleries.

a b c d

Cardhu: The original rather plain label (c) above – this one was issued for France – was replaced by oval disks, appropriate to the square bottle introduced in the late eighties (d). There have been two different versions of the latter.

Clynelish: This label (below) was used both by Gordon & MacPhail and the distillery. Sale of a miniature with 'fauna' label is restricted almost exclusively at the distillery.

a   b   c

Dalmore: An early miniature by Duncan MacBeth is very rare. After Whyte & Mackay acquired the distillery, a miniature was issued with an elaborate gold label (b). This was followed by several versions of a black label with a stag's head motif (c) which has been retained on the white label on a 'true' shape miniature.

Old Fettercairn: The first label issued by Whyte & Mackay on the 'unaged' malt, featured an archway (a). A rather insipid pale label with a view of the distillery followed. When issued as a ten year old, the label was again changed (b).

a   b

Both Dalmore and Fettercairn first appeared as dumpy miniatures and both these and later labels were also used on plastic miniatures introduced for the airline trade.

Dalwhinnie: A special bottling of the 8 year old malt was issued for sale locally (a). An early label (b) on the 15 year old malt had a colourful picture of the distillery. This has been superseded by a true miniature of the widely promoted dumpy bottle label (c). A dark blue version of this label was used on the 1980 'Classic Malt'.

a   b   c

Glenfarclas: The older label (a) which was also used by Gordon & MacPhail has been discarded in favour of successively more colourful formats (b, c, d) using a view of the distillery but retaining the Glenfarclas 'signature'. Variations of label (d) are used for different ages (10, 15, 25, 30) and for the '105' which has no age statement.

a   b   c   d

Glenfiddich: The cartouche style label was first used for an 8 year old on a flat bottle and has varied only slightly over the years. No age is stated on the standard bottling

nor on the label of the handsome '1887 Classic'.
Glengarioch: Like the other miniatures in the Morrison stable, Auchentoshan and Bowmore, this malt has had a variety of labels, with several changes in the late nineties There was no statement of age on the fine label *(reproduced on page 63)* that graced the first dumpy green miniature Between labels (a) and (b) there was briefly a 10 year old with a striped brown label containing much information in tiny type.

a   b   c   a

Glengoyne: The first miniature of Glengoyne was a 'limited' edition of 30,000 for Italy (a) above. The dark style of this label was echoed on the first UK 8 year old issue, with two gold stills within a wreath of barley – page 56 (b). The first 10 year old label was cream with a colourful distillery picture (c). Label (d) was used for 10 and 12 year old malts; an earlier version for the 10 year old had a solid gold background.

Later the picture of the distillery was dropped and label (e) was introduced for 10 and 17 year old malts. Serious collectors of Glengoyne should look out for a 3cl version of the 17 year old (used in a promotion) and a plain label single cask miniature issued in a wooden box in 1998. A miniature of 1969 'vintage reserve' was sold with the 70cl bottle and may be more difficult to find.

b   c   d   e

Glen Grant: The most easily recognised of labels, used for many years by authorised bottlers, is still to be found on 'official' miniatures. A more modern style was introduced briefly on the 12 year old malt.

Glenlivet: The present split label is the first radical change for some time. A miniature of the 18 year old has been issued for Japan. Triffin illustrates a number of rare early labels, all used in export markets.

Glenmorangie. The label style is unmistakable. It has been constant on the 10 year old and varied only slightly for the two versions of the 18 year old label. The details for the three 'wood finish' malts are different but the family style remains.

Glen Moray: There have been four distinct label styles; Style (d) was also used with a cream background for a 15 year old malt.

a   b   c   d

Glen Ord: The product of the distillery at Muir of Ord has been marketed successively as 'Ord', 'Glenordie', illustrated on page 63 (b), and Glen Ord.

Glen Scotia: Two labels, one light olive with a rounded top on page 63 (c) and the other dark green, both feature a kilted hunter with four leashed hounds

Glenturret is to be found with a variety of label styles The first label, issued by 'sole agents', Paisley Whisky Co, was a simple affair on a gold ground. Subsequent labels issued by the distillery on 8 and 12 year old miniatures seem to have been printed in small batches, as there are many minor variations. Two later styles of label are illustrated. There is also a similar oval label for the 8, 12 and 15 year old with border in gold

Inchgower: Two labels from Bell's regime are illustrated on page 57

Isle of Jura: Label (a) was used on a flat miniature. The scaled up version (b) appeared on the first 'waisted' miniature.

a   b

Two later labels, including an insipid transparent one, feature a map of the island.

Knockando: This is a classic 'true' miniature. The label has varied only slightly since first issued and records the date of distillation.

Lagavulin: The 12 and 16 year old malts have been given markedly different labels (a) and (b) below.

a   b   c   d

Linkwood: Two styles of label are shown above. There was also a black version of (c). Both versions of (c) were on flat miniatures.

Littlemill: The label, shown on page 62 (e), was used on early miniatures and has been adapted for use on later dumpy green miniature, which has no indication of age.

Lochnagar: The label illustrated was issued with both white and gold borders. There was a third similar version on a differently shaped 'cut out' label.

Macallan The greatest scope for specialising comes from malts that are issued with the 'vintage' specified on the label. Macallan is a favourite; the 18 year old has been issued with distillation date shown since 1981 (1963 'vintage') and there are many variations of age (10, 12, 16 year old). A few labels are sufficiently different from the standard (eg: the 7 year old for Italy, the unaged 'Distiller's Choice' for Japan, the *Private Eye* issue and some rare specials) to lend extra interest.

Oban: The lozenge shaped label on the 12 year old 'perfume bottle' miniature has given way to an interesting but almost unreadable label on the 16 year old.

Springbank: No malt has been bottled at so many different ages, from 'raw' Scottish Spirit to whisky at the three year old minimum, then 5, 8, 10, 12, 15, 21, 25 and 30 year old. For many years, miniatures have been issued for the home and overseas markets with many variations, particularly on style (a) label. A variation of (b) was used on the dumpy 25 and 30 year old miniatures. Label (c)

was found on 10 and 21 year old miniatures. Two limited editions – 1952 and 1919 – had labels in style (d).

a   b   c   d

Longrow, produced at the same distillery in 1973/4, has also had a number of labels both aged and dated. There was a limited edition on a dumpy miniature of the 1973 (first distillation/last cask).

Talisker: Two labels are illustrated on page 62 (f) and (g). As with the other United Distillers' Classic Malts, there is a black label for the 'double distilled' version.

Tamdhu: The 8 year old bottling had a pleasant brown pictorial label (a) below. Its successor, with a view of the Tamdhu Burn (b), was pretty and had a poem too. More recent labels with a cut out shape, have been prosaically informative (c).

a   b   c

Tamnavulin & Tullibardine The first miniatures for these sister distilleries had elaborate cut out labels (a). While Tullibardine has had just one updated label (b) Tamnavulin has had four. Label (c) was replaced by one with a rounded top and thick green border which was followed in turn by two different rectangular labels for the 10 and 12 year old malts.

a   b   c

Tobermory The malt from the Ledaig Distillery at Tobermory has been bottled under both names. The dumpy green Tobermory miniature has a white 'fired on' label that had earlier been used for a vatted malt. A Ledaig label is illustrated on page 62 (a).

Tomatin: After being in use for many years, the label illustrated on page 62 (b) was replaced by one of similar design with much less ornamentation.

Tomintoul: The first label for this malt was a plain black one on a dumpy miniature used also for early bottlings of Fettercairn and Dalmore. This was followed by a label showing five stylised ears of barley on a flat miniature, page 62 (c). A later 10 year old malt was in a standard round miniature with a green label.

Tormore: The product of this distillery has been issued with three quite different labels. The first which was on a flat miniature is shown below (d). A second, red and black metallic, was on a true 'decanter' shape while a third is lightly coloured on a standard round miniature.

a	b	c	d

Chivas have issued two very different labels for 15 year old Longmorn; a very plain label below (h) was succeeded by a picture that places the distillery buildings in a craggy landscape with a stag and a Celtic cross.

e	f	g	h

Of the malt whiskies that have been bottled in miniature by the proprietors but not mentioned above, most have had only one label, with only minor variations.

a   b   c

Some 'Own Label' miniature labels *(see page 26)*

a   b   c

Connoisseurs Choice labels *(see page 70)*

a   b   c   d

MacArthur's labels *(see page 73)*

Limited Editions and Rare Malt Miniatures

The rarest miniature whiskies are accidental survivors from an age when these bottlings were samples, intended for consumption. There are several examples of miniatures from 'Milton Distillery' (the name was changed to Strathisla in the early fifties), including a pear-shaped bottle which is possibly the earliest malt whisky miniature surviving with contents intact. Other contenders for this title are 'Old North Esk' mentioned below and a Glenmorangie, of which only one specimen is known to exist.

Some malt miniatures owe their rarity to the fact that they were issued for export, notably for Italy. For this market, Auchentoshan was once labelled as 'Glentoshan' and there were special bottlings of, among others, Clynelish, Glenburgie, Glengoyne, Glen Scotia and Springbank miniatures.

Glentauchers was sold on the French market at 5 and 10 year old and was handsomely presented in specially shaped miniature bottles which were also used by Buchanan's for some of their deluxe blends.

Bell's sold Blair Athol and Dufftown in some overseas markets at 12 year old. A few miniatures, given away at trade fairs, have found their way back to the UK. The labels are in the *cartouche* style.

More modern rarities command greater attention

from collectors. These may be restricted labellings for specific occasions, like the special miniature of 15 year old Ardmore donated to the *Children in Need* appeal in 1988 – a rare official bottling of that malt. Others have been limited by the small amount of spirit available.

In the mid-eighties, some Springbank malt, distilled in 1919 and originally bottled at 66.3° proof, was put into 5cl bottles and issued in a numbered edition of 23. Some of the 1952 distillation from the same source appeared in a limited edition of about 40 miniatures in 1989. In the following year, Signatory Vintage marketed 30 miniatures of 1949 Macallan at a strength of 47.9% vol., with numbered and signed labels.

The remains of a cask of Royal Brackla 60 year old malt was bottled and mostly shipped to Japan in 1986. Miniatures taken from this bottling have appeared, at first not named as such but with a Buchanan's label.
Later, miniatures with what appears to be a photocopy of the larger label, have been sold at auction along with a standard sized bottle.

Some miniatures have been available only at the distillery concerned. The fine 'true' miniature of Miltonduff was given only to distillery visitors and stocks are now finished. Of even more limited availability were miniatures of Cameronbridge, Cambus, Caledonian and North of Scotland Grain Whiskies. The last three were bottled for just one 'open day'.

Some curious malt miniatures have turned up in very small quantities. The provenance of some may be suspect but most are thought to be trial runs or trade samples.

Aultmore: There are two labels on record: A plain one, showing neither age nor strength but issued officially in the US, is illustrated in Triffin. The second, with a label in the style of the current 70cl issue, has not been released commercially.

Glen Deveron: Before the proprietors of the Macduff Distillery released the current miniature, there was a small run for the French market. The label described the contents as 'unblended Scotch malt whisky from the Macduff Highland Distillery'.

Glen Esk. A miniature labelled 'Old North Esk Pot Still Whisky' may be the earliest surviving malt whisky miniature.

Glenfarclas: Some doubts were cast on the provenance of an early miniature of the handsome 25 year old bottling. There is no doubt that a series of miniatures of different ages, claiming to be of Glenfarclas and sporting the picture of an Aberdeen Angus bull were rather crude confections.

Glendronach: There are a small number of both 8 and 12 year old Glendronach in two versions; one has facsimile labels, the other plain.

Glenglassaugh: A rather mysterious miniature, originating in Italy, where a limited number of the standard bottles had been marketed.

Macallan: In 1979, the proprietors of Macallan took back direct responsibility for the bottling of *The Finest Single Malt Whisky on Speyside* – to quote the label. The occasion was marked by the issue of a miniature with an odd spiral label, which specifies neither the age nor the strength of the contents. A miniature was used to encourage retailers to promote sales of Macallan before Christmas 1994; it was never on public sale and is much sought after by collectors. The label is plain and declares the contents to be *The Macallan Scotch Whisky* at 50.6% vol., from fino butt No.10469 and distilled in 1967. A year or so earlier, a limited edition miniature 26 year old was used for promotional purposes.

Merchant Bottlings of Malt Whisky

In the early days of the industry, the bottling of malt whiskies was undertaken by merchants and not by the proprietors of the distilleries. The practice has almost disappeared. Some of the merchants, like Teacher's and Chivas Brothers have become blenders and bottlers with a large market. Others have ceased to bottle. Gordon & MacPhail continue to act as authorised bottlers on a small scale but such major distilleries as Glenfarclas, Macallan and Glenlivet now directly control this aspect of their business. The change is one result of the greater emphasis now placed on the sale of single malts and the desire of the marketing companies to have a consistent product.

The character of the whisky from any distillery undoubtedly varies from cask to cask, so that it is not possible to guarantee that the malt taken from any one cask will have the particular character desired by the proprietor. The official bottler may wish to 'lose' the contents of lesser casks in his standard product but, in doing so, he will surely also lose some very good ones. It is the enthusiast who seeks the special experience of sampling the malt from a particularly fine cask who will be the customer of a new breed of merchant bottlers. These merchants purchase casks on the open market and bottle the contents, using their own brand names but indicating the distillery of origin on the label.

Among the first to offer this kind of bottling to the general trade was Wm. Cadenhead. Gordon & MacPhail followed with their distinctive 'Connoisseurs Choice' label. Others in the field are Signatory Vintage and James MacArthur & Co. The products of these firms will be found in specialist whisky shops; all of them issue miniatures which serve as introductory samplers to what is now a very wide range of malt whiskies at interesting ages and in a variety of strengths.

Gordon & MacPhail

The Elgin firm of Gordon & MacPhail has had a long and distinguished connection with the whisky trade, in particular as bottlers of fine malts. They were also pioneers in the bottling of miniature Scotch whiskies. In the thirties they bottled the first Glen Grant miniatures in pear shaped bottles, corked and capsuled. After the war, they introduced the flask miniature which was later packaged in a tartan carton with acetate front. This 'Tartanpak' range, purchased widely as souvenirs and gifts, introduced malt whiskies into thousands of homes. The flask shape miniature has been discarded in favour of tall round miniatures and the standard range still comes in a tartan carton embossed with the familiar stag logo. They broke new ground with special labels for two royal weddings and have 5cl versions of their 50 year old Mortlach, Glenlivet and Glen Grant malts. Their 40 year old Glen Calder is the oldest blended whisky in miniature form.

The Connoisseurs Choice selection made available for tasting many of the SMD malts that had previously gone entirely to the blenders. The range of malts available has been added to regularly, through three label changes *(illustrated on page 63)*.

There is now a series of single cask bottlings at cask strength and the centenary of the firm was marked by a special bottling of eight malts in both standard and miniature bottles. In 1998, after a long absence, Macallan was again bottled (with a *'Speymalt'* heading). In the same year, five other Highland Distillers malts were issued with similar labels as *'The MacPhail's Collection'*.

The firm's commitment to the Scotch whisky industry has been sealed by their purchase, in 1993, of Benromach and its subsequent re-equiping as a distillery.

Wm Cadenhead Miniatures

William Cadenhead were Aberdeen merchants who had their own blends and bottled some malts, including Laphroaig and Ardbeg, with uniform black labels. Since the firm moved its operating base to Campbeltown, where it is closely associated with Springbank, they have bottled the products of many other distilleries, some at unusual ages, using the same distinctive labelling.

In 1979, Wm Cadenhead issued a set of 12 miniatures, all at 80° proof, including a first bottling of St Magdalene. This was the first time that well matured malts – Highland Park and Mortlach both at 22 year old – were made available in a form convenient for sampling. A second batch of 12, all aged 17 years or more, followed in 1983.

Further miniatures appeared in retail shops every two years or so until 1995, when there was a change in label style. Another type of label was issued for an 'Original Collection' (which correspond almost exactly in age and strength with earlier issues). Five miniatures containing Scotch grain whiskies were issued with the same style of label but in a different colour.

First issue　　　　*'Original' issue*　　　　*1995 change*

In addition to the miniatures that have appeared on general sale, others have been sold through the firm's own outlets in Campbeltown, Edinburgh and London. Yet more have been issued for outlets in the USA. These limited bottlings seem to have been made specifically to meet a demand from ardent collectors for 'something different' and in some cases it would appear that they are limited refills from 75cl bottles. Dedicated collectors may like to know that these special bottlings included the first issue in miniature of Ladyburn and Teaninich malts.

Signatory Vintage

The Edinburgh Firm, Signatory Vintage, bottles many fine malts and most of them appear in miniature as well as in standard formats. Two basic styles of label have been used, and give very detailed information. The 'vintage' year is highlighted but the date of distillation, the month bottled and the age at bottling are also noted. The type of cask and its number are recorded. The size of the edition is shown and each label is hand numbered.

Signatory, like Cadenhead and MacArthur, undertake private bottlings. These have usually had specially designed labels and some – like the two sets for the Scottish Wildlife Trust – have been on general sale. However, a number of special bottlings for outlets in the USA have used the standard type of label.

From 1997, Signatory has produced special limited editions of rare malts from 'Silent Stills'. Included along with the standard bottle is a miniature with the same distinctive labelling and a disc cut from the cask from which the bottles were filled.

James MacArthur & Co

The miniatures that were initially bottled by James MacArthur & Co were all malts at 12 years of age and all were at cask strength. The original labels were uniformly plain but the information given was particularly clear. Along with the more usual details, the cask number was shown but not the year of filling. These first miniatures were primarily samplers for malts available in standard bottles

Later issues of miniatures are almost certainly aimed at the collector. The label was changed, becoming less dull and having a pretty picture of a still. Usually both the age of the whisky and the date of distillation are shown and some bottlings are at 43% or 40% vol. The cask number no longer appears. A further label variation appeared in 1997 when two miniatures, designated as 'Old Master's Cask Strength Selection' were issued.

The 500th anniversary of the Scotch whisky industry was celebrated in 1994 and many firms issued special labels. MacArthur's were most prolific in the field, issuing 16 miniatures over a two year period.

The four styles of label are illustrated on page 63. In addition to the miniatures which have been sold in shops, MacArthur labels have appeared on 'private' bottlings. Some of these have been in sets for the Mini Bottle Club. Others were for overseas outlets. Yet more have been specially issued for individual collectors and seem to have been refilled from 70cl bottles obtained from various sources. Some collectors now consider such miniatures to be unworthy of their interest.

Other 'Unofficial' Bottlings

Macfarlane Bruce and Co, Inverness, with their 'As We Get It' label, have marketed Balvenie, Macallan and Aberlour at cask strength. The first two have been sold in 5cl bottles.

Some individual shops with access to casks have arranged for malt whiskies to be bottled for sale in their own outlets. Cairngorm Whisky Centre in Aviemore, The Whisky Castle in Tomintoul and Royal Mile Whiskies in Edinburgh are three that have their own miniatures.

The Scotch Malt Whisky Society bottles selected malt whiskies obtained on the open market. Full sized bottles are filled at cask strength and are sold only to members. From time to time the society has also filled miniatures, but at reduced strength, as samplers. Sales of the 5cl bottles are also limited to members.

Three firms that sell direct to the public through 'membership' schemes are 'Blackadder', 'Master of Malt' and 'The Whisky Connoisseur'.

A Malt by any other name…

In 1994, collectors were confronted with a new name among malt whiskies. Not a new whisky, though bottled by Signatory Vintage, this malt had been distilled in 1972 and the name stencilled on the cask was Killyloch. The story is that this cask contained the product of a second still at Inver House Distillery at Moffat (the first was the source of Glenflagler malt) and had been intended for use in blending. It is said that the whisky was to be called 'Lillyloch', in honour of the water source on the outskirts of Airdrie, but the stencil cutter got his spelling wrong and, perhaps to save the expense of cutting another stencil, the name was retained.

In the seventies, Springbank Distillery produced a heavily peated malt that was quite different from their usual product. To avoid confusion among tasters, this malt was given the name of a distillery that shared the site in the nineteenth century – Longrow.

The present Brora Distillery was called Clynelish until 1969 when the name was transferred to a new distillery built alongside it.

The distillery built in recent years near Kingussie on the south bank of the River Spey is called 'Speyside'. When the malt was first bottled in 1995, it was called 'Drumguish' (after the nearby hamlet), because the name 'Speyside' had already been used to designate another product.

Knockdhu is the name of the distillery built at Knock, Banffshire in 1893 and its product was so named until 1995. In that year, to avoid confusion with the more widely known bottled malt from Knockando, the name of the product was changed to 'An Cnoc'

The official bottling of the Macduff Distillery bears the name 'Glen Deveron'.

The present Strathisla-Glenlivet Distillery was founded in 1786 as Milltown. It was later known as Milton. The name 'Strathisla' was used from 1870-90 and the Milton name was finally dropped after the distillery came into Seagram's hands in the 1950s. To add a little confusion, there was – briefly – in the 1820s, a distillery known as Strathisla, probably on the same site as the present Strathmill Distillery.

Miniatures labelled 'Glencraig' and 'Mosstowie' contain the products of special shaped stills installed at Glenburgie and Miltonduff distilleries respectively

Inchmurrin and Rhosdhu are in effect trade names for the output of Loch Lomond Distillery

The malt from the distillery at Muir of Ord has been bottled variously as 'Ord', 'Glenordie' and (now) 'Glen Ord'.

Collecting Blended Scotch Whisky

The scope for specialising within the sphere of blended Scotch whiskies is not so great as for the malts. A number of possibilities have been mentioned on page 14 and have been enlarged upon elsewhere. One of the most interesting fields is that of product promotion: it is often possible to identify the whisky used and this lends additional interest. Other categories may be so frustratingly open ended that only the most dedicated collector will pursue them.

Some collectors have assembled quite large numbers of label variations of common brands. The overseas market is a fruitful hunting ground for the likes of *Johnnie Walker*, *Black and White* and *Dewar's*. The specialists in particular brands also tend to branch out into the realm of 'go withs' – mainly advertising materials, from table mats to water jugs and figurines.

Keeping a Record

The number of miniatures available keeps growing and there are regular changes in label details that are of interest to the serious collector.

Few people have the capacity to remember all details, so, as soon as a collector 'comes out' and finally admits his or her affliction, it is advisable to prepare a comprehensive record. This should cover not only the miniatures already possessed but also a 'wants' list

If the collector has access to equipment, a photographic record is ideal. Otherwise, as full as possible description of each container and label should be entered against each distillery or brand name. An indexed notebook or a card system is vital for speedy reference .

The Mini Bottle Club

Collectors of miniature whiskies wishing to learn more about their hobby and seeking contact with others with a similar interest, may want to join the Mini Bottle Club, the only such organisation in the United Kingdom. Details can be obtained by sending a stamped addressed envelope to the membership secretary:–

> David Hamilton
> 47 Burradon Road
> Burradon
> CRAMLINGTON
> NE23 7NF

The club covers all liquors found in small bottles but the main focus of attention is on Scotch whisky. There is a bimonthly newsletter which covers all aspects of collecting; it includes illustrations of miniatures old and new and has had some useful in-depth articles on individual distilleries and brands.

Members of the Mini Bottle Club hold periodic meetings. These social gatherings are the occasion for the exchange of information and the swapping of bottles. The club also organises regular postal auctions.

Triffin: An important source of information for the collector is the American publication *The Whiskey Miniature Bottle Collection* by James A Triffin. Volume 2 covers Scotch whisky and illustrates many of the miniatures issued in the United States from the end of prohibition to 1981.

Hunting Miniature Whiskies

Miniature whiskies may legally be sold only from licensed premises. Such licences restrict sales on Sundays.

Many Scottish gift shops now sell miniatures and some have comprehensive selections. Even specialist shops, such as those listed in the next section, will not have discontinued versions of the more popular brands in stock for long after they have been replaced. There is no market place for older issues except through contact with fellow collectors. Postal auctions of miniature bottles is organised regularly by the Mini Bottle Club *(see page 79)*.

Two places where the miniature hunter is least likely to be able to buy are distilleries that do not have a visitor centre (and this means *most* distilleries) and the sales offices of blending companies. Most of the distilleries that cater for visitors now have comprehensive stocks of their own products as well as souvenir items relating to them. Sometimes the distillery may be the only source in the UK of particular miniatures – eg: miniature flagons and certain Wm Grant bottlings, like Robbie Dhu and Black Barrel, at Glenfiddich and their own 'true' miniature at Miltonduff.

Another point to remember is that if you cannot find a particular miniature in specialist shops, the original supplier will have exhausted his stocks long before.

Buyer's Guide

Most off-licence stores and many retail gift shops stock miniatures of the popular brands only. The traveller in Scotland will find specialist shops in most tourist centres but there are only a few outlets with really comprehensive stocks where you are likely to get knowledgeable help from the proprietor or his assistants. There follows a list of retail establishments that are known to offer a good service for the collector. Some publish lists and will sell by mail order.

Many Scottish souvenir shops now sell miniatures of the more popular malt and blended whiskies. Those listed below carry better than average stocks.

SCOTLAND

Aboyne – *George Strachan & Co*, licensed grocers in the Station Square and with several branches on Deeside, is an old established whisky specialist, with plenty of miniatures including some 'own labels'.

Edinburgh – *Royal Mile Whiskies* has many miniatures, including malts bottled under the 'Dram Good Whisky' label. Also *The Whisky Shop*, Waverley Market and *Cadenheads Whisky Shop*, in the Canongate, who stock mostly their own label miniatures.

Elgin – *Gordon & MacPhail*, long established merchants and bottlers of fine malt whiskies, have a retail shop in South Street where they have a comprehensive display of miniatures. They issue mail order lists.

Fort William – *Peter MacLennan* and *The Whisky Shop*

Glasgow – *Robin Hood Gift House*

Nr Huntly – *The Grouse Inn*, Cabrach, has a large and interesting collection of standard bottles on display and has a good stock of miniatures for sale.

Inverary – *Loch Fyne Whiskies*

Inverness – *The Whisky Shop*, Bridge Street

Oban – *Cheese and Wine Shop*

Pitlochry – *Highland House* has a large stock of novelties as well as miniatures. Also *Robertson's Supermarket*, has a good stock of miniatures and a mail order service.

Tomintoul – *The Whisky Castle* has an excellent selection of standard and miniature bottles.

Tyndrum – *Whisky Galore*

ENGLAND
Lincoln – *The Whisky Shop*, Bailgate

London – *Harrod's*, Knightsbridge. Their stock of miniatures is limited but includes some of their own bottling.

Newcastle upon Tyne – *Fenwick's*, Northumberland Street have a wide selection of miniatures.

Further Reading

There is an ever growing body of literature on the subject of Scotch whisky. In seeking information, the reader needs to be wary because there have been many changes in structure and ownership, during the last 20 years. However, the process of making whisky has hardly changed and some straightforward accounts are to be found in the publicity literature of the major companies.

Many of the earlier studies of the whisky industry are no longer of interest to the ordinary reader but the following have attained the status of classics:

Sir Robert Bruce Lockhart – *Scotch, The Whisky of Scotland in Fact and Story* – A personal study by one whose roots were in Speyside
Neil Gunn – *Whisky & Scotland*
J Marshall Robb – *Scotch Whisky* (Chambers 1950)
A delightful book with a foreword by Maurice Walsh and drawings by George Mackie

Some more up-to-date general guides are:
Michael Brander – *Essential Guide to Scotch Whisky*
Charles MacLean – *Pocket Whisky Book*
Roddy Martine – *Scotland: The Land and Whisky*
Michael Moss – *Scotch Whisky*
Jim Murray – *Complete Book of Whisky*
J Wilson – *Scotland's Malt Whiskies*
Derek Cooper – *The Little Book of Malt Whisky*
S & J Cribb – *Whisky on the Rocks*

Two recent anthologies of whisky literature are:

Derek Cooper – *A Taste of Scotch*
David Daiches – *A Wee Dram*.

Although the information given is now a bit out-of-date, there are many useful facts about the whisky industry in its commercial aspects in:

Philip Morrice – *The Schweppes Guide to Scotch*

Two comprehensive surveys of the Scotch whisky industry of recent years are:

H Charles Craig – *Scotch Whisky Industry Record*
Moss and Hume – *The Making of Scotch Whisky*
This fully annotated and well illustrated book is a worthy successor to Alfred Barnard's classic *The Whisky Distilleries of the United Kingdom* (originally published in 1887, reprinted by Mainstream in 1987 and also, covering surviving Scottish distilleries, by Famedram)

Writers have often been tempted to pontificate about their favourite malts but a new trend was set when *Decanter* magazine published its *Harrod's Book of Whiskies* which detailed the findings of a panel of pundits. Now the reader has a choice of three more oracles to consult:

Michael Jackson – *Malt Whisky Companion*
Wallace Milroy – *Malt Whisky Almanac*
Lamont and Tucek – *The Malt Whisky File*

The Future for Miniature Whiskies

The whisky trade is never static and the supply of miniatures is always changing. Familiar labels may disappear but there will be new ones to fill the gap. Collectors constantly seek out new labels and the demand generated by this expanding hobby should help persuade the whisky companies to develop further this aspect of their promotional activities. The more miniatures that are produced by the traditional whisky trade, the less scope there will be for those fringe operators who take advantage of the constant demand for new labels. Indeed, with some companies guided by experts who see periodic change as a key to marketing success, there seems little danger that the supply of new labels will dry up.

The use of miniatures for sampling malts has been encouraged by some of the larger companies – for example, United Distillers and Glenmorangie – who sell sets of miniatures with tasting notes. There is no doubt that the growing band of enthusiasts who wish to broaden the spectrum of their tasting experience, will welcome the availability of miniatures as a convenient and cheap guide to further purchase.

Late in 1998, Springbank announced the issue of a series of well aged malts in 70cl bottles. When the issue is complete, purchasers will be able to claim a set of miniatures of these bottles. Perhaps miniature specialists will reverse the logical procedure by using the larger bottles as tasting samplers, retaining the miniatures in their collection

There is much scope for widening the use of miniatures for special labelling. Several distilling firms (notably Morrison Bowmore and Springbank) have been willing to make their malts available for this purpose. It is desirable that this practice should be more encouraged by the legitimate trade, which could benefit through association with good causes and selective product development. Easy access to cheap printing encourages the re-labelling of miniatures to commemorate special events, for fund raising and for product promotion and all too often this is done in an amateurish way and without regard to the quality of the whisky used.

In the long run, it is the people who buy miniatures who will most influence the way the trade will develop. Knowledgeable and selective purchasing, whether by consumer or collector, is the key to the future of miniature whiskies.

Distillery Index

(*For explanation of abbreviations, please see page 91*)

Malt Distilleries

	CC	G&M	McA	SVint	Cad	
Aberfeldy	P	abc		bc	b	23 45 48
Aberlour	P			a	a	16 22 47 50
Allt-á-Bhainne			b	b		46
An Cnoc – *see under Knockdhu*						
Ardbeg	P	abc		ab	ab	48 50
Ardmore	p		b	bc	ab	46 65
Auchentoshan	P					31 47 50 64
Auchroisk	P				a	44 50
Aultmore	p			b		45 48 66
Balblair	P		abd			16 48
Balmenach		ab		b	c	b	48
Balvenie	P			abc	b	16 19 47 51
Banff		ab			b	b	45
Ben Nevis	P	ab		b?	b	ab	48
Benriach	P	ab	c		b	b	46
Benrinnes		abc	d	c	ab	ac	44
Benromach	P	ab		b	b	48 70
Ben Wyvis						47
Bladnoch	P	c		bc	ab	a	45 51
Blair Athol	P			bc		ac	23 44 51 64
Bowmore	P			b	ab	16 31 47 51
Braes of Glenlivet				b	b	46
(renamed Braeval)						
Brora		bc			b	45 75
Bruichladdich	P		c	d	ab		47 52
Bunnahabhain	P		f	bc	a		47
Caol Ila		abc	cd	abc	ab	ab	44
Caperdonich		ab			ac		46
Cardhu	P					16 22 44 52
Clynelish	P	c	ab		b	ab	23 31 44 53 64
Coleburn		ab		bc		b	26 45
Convalmore		abc		b	b	ab	45

	CC	G&M	McA	SVint	Cad	
Cragganmore	P	abc			b		44
Craigellachie	P	abc		a	a	a	45 48
Dailuaine		ab		ab		a	44
Dallas Dhu		abc	b		ab		44
Dalmore	P				b	b	16 47 53
Dalwhinnie	P	ab				b	20 44 54
Deanston	P				a		48
Drumguish	P						48 75
Dufftown	P		ab		b		26 44 51 64
Edradour	P	a			ab	a	47
Fettercairn	P						47 53
Glen Albyn		abc			ab		45
Glenallachie	P				b		47
Glenburgie	p		bcd				46 64
Glencraig		ab					76
Glencadam		abc				a	46
Glendronach	P		a		abc		46 62 67
Glendullan	P			b	b	abc	44
Glen Elgin	P				b	ab	44
Glenesk	P	b				b	45 66
Glenfarclas	P		ab		ab	ab	19 27 30
							48 54 66
Glenfiddich	P					ab	47 54
Glen Flagler	P				a		48
Killyloch					a		75
Glengarioch	P						23 47 55 63
Glenglassaugh				b		abc	47 67
Glengoyne	P						31 47 55 64
Glen Grant	P		ab		ab	ab	29 46 56
Glen Keith	P	a		bcd	a	b	46
Glenkinchie	P					a	44
Glenlivet	P		abc		ab	ac	43 46 56
Glenlochy		abc				ab	45
Glenlossie		abc		ab	b	b	44
Glen Mhor			abc		ab		45

	Cad	CC	G&M	McA	S.Vint
Glenmorangie	P				30 48 56 64
Glen Moray	P			a	48 57
Glen Ord	P			ab	44 57 63 76
Glenrothes	P	abdf	b	ab	47
Glen Scotia	P	ac	a	ab	48 57 63 64
Glen Spey			b	b	44
Glentauchers	*p*		b	b	46 64
Glenturret	P	f	abc	ac	47 57
Glenugie		a		b	46
Glenury Royal		ab	ab	ac	45
Highland Park	P	acdf	ab	abc	47
Imperial	ab	b	ab	ac b	46
Inchgower	P			b	44 58
Inverleven			b		46
Isle of Arran	P	*see text*			37 48
Isle of Jura	P		b	b	47 58
Kininvie					47
Kinclaith		ab		a	46
Knockdhu	P	ab			76
An Cnoc	P				48 76
Knockando	P				16 20 44 47 58
Ladyburn					47
Lagavulin	P			b	44 58
Laphroaig	P	a		b	46
Ledaig	P	ab	b	b b	48 62
Tobermory					61
Linkwood	P	ab	bc	ab ab	44 58
Littlemill	P			b	48 58 62 63
Loch Lomond					48 76
Inchmurrin	P			b	76
Rhosdhu	P			b	76
Lochside		a		ac	48
Longmorn	P	abc	ab	a	46 62
Macallan	P	ae	abc	ab	16 20 23 26 47 59 67

	CC	G&M	McA	Svint	Cad	
Macduff						
Glen Deveron	P	ab		bcd	b	b	48 66 76
Mannochmore		b				b	44
Millburn		abc		b	b	b	45
Miltonduff	P	ab	b		bc		46 65
Mosstowie		abc					76
Mortlach			abd	b	bc	ab	44 69
North Port		ab				b	45
Oban	P						16 23 44 59
Pittyvaich				ab		ac	44
Port Ellen		abc	c	a	abc	b	45
Pulteney	P		ab				22 48
Rosebank	P	bc		b	ab	a	45
Royal Brackla	p	abc		a	b		45 48 65
Royal Lochnagar	P	a					44 59
St Magdalene		c	d			ab	45
Scapa	P		ab		b	a	46
Speyburn	P	ab		c		ac	48
Springbank	P			ab	ab	ab	31 42 48 59 60 64 65
Longrow	P				b		60 75
Strathisla	P	abc				b	46 64 76
Strathmill				b	bc		44
Talisker	P	ac			b		44 60
Tamdhu	P	af			b		23 47 60
Tamnavulin	P					a	47 61
Teaninich	P			b	b	b	44
Tobermory *see Ledaig*							
Tomatin	P	abc			a	a	48 61 62
Tomintoul	P		b	a			47 61 62
Tormore	P						22 46 62
Tullibardine	P						47

90

Grain Distilleries

	CC	G&M	McA	SVint	Cad	
Ben Nevis			b?			46
Caledonian	p			c		37 45
Cambus	p			c		45
Cameronbridge	p		c			37 45
Carsebridge		c				45
Dumbarton			a	c		46
Girvan				c		37 47
Invergordon	P					37
Lochside		c		c		48
Moffat (Inver House)						48
North British	p		ab			
North of Scotland						37
Strathmore						37 45
Port Dundas						37 45
Strathclyde						46

Abbreviations used above

P	Commercially bottled in by the proprietors
p	Other 'Official' bottlings (including limited runs)
CC	**Connoisseurs Choice** *(see pages 63 and 70)*

    a Original Label   b Map Label
    c Revised Map label

G&M   **Gordon & MacPhail** *(see pages 69-70)*
    a Tartanpak flask   b Tartanpak Tall Round
    c Cask Strength   d Centenary issue
    e 'Speymalt' label   f 'MacPhail's Collection'

McA   **MacArthur** *(see page 73)*
    a Original label   b 'Still' label
    c '500' label   d 'Old Master' label

SVint   **Signatory Vintage** *(see page 72)*
    a 'S' label   b Barrel label c Other

Cad   **Cadenhead** *(see page 71)*
    a Original label   b Part 'fired on' label
    c Olive (malts) orange (grain)

The Rale Last Drappie
and
Wee Deoch an Dorus
O' Pre War
Scots Usquaebaugh
Mauted Brewed
Stilled and Preed
August 1914

by J Dewar
Perth

from the label on a miniature decanter,
sealed with a tartan ribbon and contained
along wih a pack of cards in a leather 'book'
entitled Golden Treasury